KU-280-862

CONTENTS

Selecting Your Tortoise

The choice of pets available today is enormous: dogs, cats, canaries, hamsters, parrots, ferrets, iguanas, etc., etc., etc. Moreover, most of these animals were specifically bred to keep us company. The situation with tortoises is vastly different. None of the tortoises currently available through pet shops have been bred in captivity. They were (and still are) caught in their respective native country. There they invariably were stuffed into boxes, crates, and sacks like potatoes to be dispatched on a long and agonizing journey. Many were dead on arrival at their destination. Others were weakened to such a degree that only an immediate super effort was able to pull them through. Unfortunately, this is usually not available, so even more animals die before the remainder are finally sold. And what happens to the ones sold? It is generally assumed that at the most 10% of the initial survivors will last their first year in captivity. Certainly this is nothing to be proud of!

Yet for years, even decades, the re-supply of imported tortoises was maintained so that tortoise fanciers (especially in Europe) never really had to worry about it. Every year, right on time in early summer, there were tortoises available in all sizes. The smallest were so cheap that a child could afford one from his or her pocket money. Most of these tortoises sold in Europe (usually *Testudo hermanni*, the Greek tortoise or Hermann's tortoise) came from countries around the Mediterranean Sea, primarily from Greece. Consequently, the "Greek tortoise" became a permanent item among tortoise fanciers.

FACING PAGE: A leopard tortoise, *Geochelone pardalis*, is a species distributed in southern and eastern Africa. In its natural habitat this tortoise eats mainly succulents and grasses.

Today Greek tortoises are rarely ever available. They can no longer be exported from their native countries because in some areas they have become virtually extinct. Regrettably, though, there has not been a corresponding decline in the demand for tortoises. Consequently, other species are now "in." A few years ago there were the four-toed tortoises, also sometimes referred to as Russian tortoises. They come from Iran, Afghanistan, and Pakistan. When the importation of these tortoises was prohibited, the American box turtles (Europeans call them box tortoises) replaced them on the European market. These unfortunate creatures come from the United States and are even more difficult to keep than four-toed tortoises. There was wholesale death among these animals in captivity.

Only we, as buyers, can do something for tortoises. After all, each tortoise sold will necessitate the collection of more animals in the wild. Remember, from 100 animals caught, only ten will ultimately survive. This stern warning may give rise to the reader's suspicion that I am fundamentally against keeping tortoises. You will quickly see that this is not the case at all, because it indeed can be a stroke of luck for a tortoise to be looked after by someone who cares. Even if a species of tortoise is protected in its native country, there it is still only worth a fly on the wall; i.e., nothing. Children may use them for target practice, throwing stones at them. Large numbers are killed by cars on roads or by insecticides and pesticides. If a farmer finds a tortoise in his melon patch he will not hesitate to kill the animal. There are even reports that tons of tortoises have been used in the production of turtle soup.

These are enough reasons for all of us to treasure each tortoise in our care, not as just a recreational hobby but instead as a genuine contribution to the nature conservation that we all talk about!

In reality, the approach to keeping a tortoise must be like this:

—Give careful consideration to whether you really want a tortoise or whether some other animal will do instead!

—Read up on tortoise care to find out whether you will be able to care properly for such an animal, possibly for many years!

Testudo graeca is a tortoise known as the Mediterranean spur-thighed tortoise and Moorish tortoise. In spite of its specific name it is not found in Greece.

—If you have a tortoise already and wish to get rid of it, DO NOT simply release it! Approach an animal protection organization or a terrarium club and they will often place the animal with someone who can look after it.

—If you notice that you are very good in keeping tortoises DO NOT start a collection of many species. Instead, attempt to breed animals of one or a few species.

—Try to establish contact with other tortoise fanciers in your neighborhood to share mutually beneficial information about your animals.

—Finally, freely exchange or loan out tortoises to increase the probability of breeding success in captivity.

Useful Information

Tortoises (and of course turtles in general) are reptiles. As such they are related to lizards, crocodiles, and (as unlikely as it may seem) snakes. The most conspicuous mutual character shared by all these groups is their scaly skin. In tortoises this is only visible on the legs, head, and tail. The largest part of the body is encased by the shell, the carapace on top and the plastron below. It consists on the outside of large horny scales that are present in distinct patterns. The shell provides the tortoise with an effective protection against many enemies, so it can afford to be slow and peaceful. When in danger tortoises simply retreat into their "house" and then wait until the danger has passed. In today's street traffic this tactic has proven to be dangerous—shells cannot protect a tortoise from automobiles.

The shell consists of two layers. On the outside are the horny scales or plates, and on the inside are bones firmly fused together and with the horny plates. The entire shell contains a network of blood vessels and nerves, so injuries to the carapace will cause bleeding and pain. It is easy to imagine the essential problems of growth processes in tortoises: shell and bones must always grow at the same rate.

It is easy to see how the shell grows. Each scale or plate has a small "nucleus" surrounded by concentric rings. The nucleus is the size of the scale present in a newly hatched tortoise. If we take a good look at such a scale from the shell, we notice that the nucleus is really not in the center of the adult plate. There has obviously been differential growth along the various sides of the scale. This reflects the way a tortoise's

FACING PAGE: Frontal view of a Greek tortoise, *Testudo hermanni*. This species was once the most popular pet tortoise in Europe. However, it is now considered an endangered species and is no longer available commercially.

The highly arched carapace of the margined tortoise, *Testudo marginata*, is evident in this adult specimen.

shell changes with time, from the roundish baby tortoise up to the more elongated, highly arched carapace of the margined tortoise (*Testudo marginata*).

The growth rings on the tortoise's scales are an important indicator of the animal's health. They show by how much the animal has grown and whether the shell has lately been adequately supplied with sufficient protein, calcium, vitamins, and UV radiation. If this has not been the case, the horny plates and the bones underneath will be so soft that the entire carapace can be compressed with one hand.

Not indicated by the growth rings is the age of a tortoise. Unlike trees, these do not represent annual growth. In years of a poor food supply these rings can be so narrow that they are hardly visible, and in good years there even may be two distinct rings.

As useful as the shell is, it also has natural disadvantages: it makes the animals heavy and clumsy. A tortoise turned on its back has difficulties getting back on its feet, and until the animal has accomplished this it is substantially more defenseless than other animals. The tortoise's legs are not very flexible, because they developed essentially only as supporting columns that push the body forward. They are not really usable for more delicate tasks. For instance, tortoises do not practice any kind of grooming behavior.

Like that of other reptiles, the metabolism of tortoises is dependent upon external temperatures. They are essentially restricted to warmer latitudes because their body temperature (and, of course, all metabolic functions) is dependent upon the

The growth rings in the horny plates of this Greek tortoise are quite distinct. Counting the growth lines presents very little difficulty.

external (ambient) temperature. Only when tortoises are warm are they able to move, feed, digest, and grow. The lower the outside temperature the less active they become, and their feeding drive also declines. At very low temperatures they become virtually rigid and their metabolic functions take place at a slow-motion tempo. At certain times this condition is quite normal, such as during natural rest periods such as hibernation and estivation, but if it goes on for too long the animals will die.

Equally lethal are temperatures that go above or below certain limits. Reptiles can die rather quickly of heat prostration, while death due to super-cooling takes somewhat longer. The basic problem here is that reptiles can not perspire, a mechanism that in warm-blooded animals serves to cool off the body; neither can they tremble, which would contribute to an increase in muscle temperature. Reptiles regulate their body temperature simply by moving in and out of the sun or shade. Moreover, the heat taken up can also be stored by the reptilian body for a certain period of time. It has to be remembered, though, that the overall intensity and maximum exposure time of solar radiation vary substantially between northern and southern latitudes. The smaller an animal is, the quicker its body warms up when exposed to the sun. The massive bodies of tortoises require a fairly long time until they are warmed up to maximum metabolic activity. The sun in northern latitudes during spring and fall will have almost set before a tortoise would be adequately warmed. Consequently, anything they may have eaten during the short warm period at midday will remain undigested in the intestine during the long cold period. This is one reason snakes (with relatively small bodies) are common in northern latitudes while tortoises are absent.

The sun is even more important in the life of tortoises for the perpetuation of the species. Tortoises deposit their eggs in the ground in selected sites that appear to them instinctively suitable: soft soil, nice and warm, not too damp and not too dry. In their native habitats such minimal parental care is sufficient to assure that the eggs develop properly and the young hatch normally. Generally, these conditions are found in areas where there is no rain for three months and a ground temperature of 86°F. In northern latitudes, however, not even the most favorable geographical areas offer these conditions.

Opinions on the intelligence of tortoises vary widely. I believe it is hardly possible to assess the intelligence of an animal that is not being kept under natural conditions and of which little is known about its normal types of behavior. Over the years I have changed my opinion on this subject several times, always in favor of the tortoises!

It is easy to observe that eyes and nose play a significant part in the orientation of tortoises. For instance, food is recognized over a distance initially by its shape and color, but only close up is the animal capable of distinguishing a red rubber ball from a tomato. On the other hand, the hearing capability of tortoises is often argued about. No doubt they are less likely to hear the footsteps of their attendant than they are

This is a common box turtle, *Terrapene carolina*, that is enjoying a stroll in the garden on a sunny day.

likely to detect vibrations through the ground. Nevertheless, I am under the impression that the animals can indeed distinguish my voice from that of others. When I am calling my animals with "co . . me," "co . . me," they indeed approach me expecting to be fed. Yet if a stranger calls the animals do not respond at all.

The well-defined senses of time and orientation in tortoises are amazing. Even after their winter hibernation they still remember when and where they have been fed. They also recognize their enclosure and they are apparently aware of any changes in it. Even last year's weak point in the fence is remembered next summer and used again for a renewed attempt to escape.

One thing is certain: tortoises do not emit any sounds. Only during copulation will the males give off more or less squeaking sounds. Apart from that tortoises can create a lot of

13

noise, such as when a tortoise is trying to "burrow" in an empty wooden crate. The animal will stop only when the claws are worn down to the flesh or when a compassionate keeper gives them some hay. Courtship fights among males for a female also tend to be quite noisy. The muffled sound of one carapace impacting on another can be heard through closed doors and windows. Between bouts the female is bitten on her legs, occasionally drawing blood. In spite of that—or possibly because of it—the female eventually submits to copulation.

Persistence and perseverance are two very characteristic traits of tortoises. They are substitutes for the lack of agility and mobility. It never ceases to amaze me where the animals manage to get to if they are sufficiently determined and are given enough time. Therefore, it is of paramount importance that the fence around the enclosure must be solidly built without any weak spots!

Tortoises can not swim, but they do like to bathe, prefererrably in clean, shallow water. However, I am always surprised to observe how quickly they soil their drinking and bathing water with feces. Here the tortoise seems to succumb to some innate instinct, even though water is never in abundance in its native habitat. This defecation instinct while bathing can be taken advantage of in the care of tortoises. In order to get "clean" animals, they are simply bathed long enough in shallow, lukewarm water (82°F).

All tortoises have individual "personalities." No two animals are ever totally alike, either in carapace markings or in behavior. They are also quite capable of adjusting to their human caretaker far more than one would imagine. After all, tortoises are very curious animals and they like quiet company. Some animals like to sit on someone's lap, having the underside of their neck scratched. Others prefer to sleep on a couch in the evening. Still others prefer to be fed by hand.

Personally, I do not prefer these extremely close contacts with the animals because then they tend to become too imprinted on humans. Instead, I spend much time observing my animals. After having kept tortoises for more than 20 years, I am still intrigued by their behavior, their preferences, and their rel tionships among each other.

View from the rear of a male Greek tortoise (top) and a female Mediterranean tortoise (bottom). Note the spur on the thigh of the tortoise below and the fused supracaudal scutes of the tortoise on the bottom.

When we receive an unknown tortoise we first have to find out what species it is. Only then will we be able to determine what the animal needs: what sort of habitat it comes from, what sort of enclosure we have to provide, what temperature it requires, what sort of food must be given, and whether the animal must hibernate during the winter months.

Who is Who?

The most important question that must be answered is: is the animal a real tortoise or some sort of aquatic turtle? The shape of the shell is not a reliable indicator, but legs and feet are good distinguishing characteristics. *Tortoises* (here extended to include American box turtles, *Terrapene*) have stout legs and feet that are virtually never clearly delineated from the legs. The claws are barely movable. To me the hind legs of tortoises are somewhat reminiscent of tiny elephant legs. *Aquatic turtles*, on the other hand, have very flexible legs with rudder-like feet and movable claws. Depending upon the species, webs for swimming are developed between the toes. How indicative the legs of a tortoise or turtle are of its habitat can be seen in box turtles. These animals are partly terrestrial and partly aquatic, and they have legs that look like a cross between those of true tortoises and those of aquatic turtles.

The following are a few brief "profiles" of familiar tortoises. All of these species are still occasionally available because of their considerable longevity and new importations. Close scrutiny of these summaries will quickly reveal that there are considerable differences in the care and maintenance requirements from species to species.

FACING PAGE: Tortoises are not boring creatures; On the contrary they are quite entertaining. An owner can expect many years of satisfaction keeping a tortoise. Unless abused or neglected, a tortoise can survive in captivity for many years.

WE'LL BURS
THE BUBBLE
...n-Bru set for Coke ba...

RD RINTOUL PET CARE CENTRE

SCOTLAND'S NO.1 SPECIALIST REPTILE OUTLET

HATCHLING SNAKES
Various Corns, King Snakes
& Western Hognoses

VARIETY OF TORTOISES
Marginated, Hermanns, Spur-
Thighed & African Spur-Thighed

MARINES, INVERTS AND HARD & SOFT CORALS

Also Available:
- Kittens • Rabbits • Guinea Pigs • Tropical Fish
- Cold Water Fish • Full Range of Accessories
& much, much more

Tel: 01506 654969
67 SOUTHBRIDGE ST., BATHGATE, WEST LOTHIAN
Visit our website www.RDRintoul-jskdm.met. OPEN SUNDAY 1PM-4PM

Greek Tortoise or Hermann's Tortoise
Testudo hermanni

SIZE: To 20 cm (8 in).

CHARACTERISTICS: Plate over base of tail (supracaudal scute) divided; tail with horny spine at tip; plastron with two wide black bands.

DISTRIBUTION: Mediterranean countries of Europe; dry brushland.

TEMPERATURE RANGE: 68–86°F (20–30°C).

WINTER HIBERNATION: Yes.

DIET: Primarily herbivorous (plant material); will eat meat only occasionally.

Moorish Tortoise, Mediterranean Spur-thighed Tortoise
Testudo graeca

SIZE: To 30 cm (12 in).

CHARACTERISTICS: Tail plate not divided; horny spur on inner thighs of hind legs; plastron with black blotches.

DISTRIBUTION: Mediterranean North Africa, Spain, Greece and Balkans to Iran.

TEMPERATURE RANGE: 68–86°F (20–30°C).

WINTER HIBERNATION: Yes.

DIET: Primarily herbivorous (plant material); meat eaten only occasionally.

Moorish Tortoise, Mediterranean Spur-thighed Tortoise, *Testudo graeca*.

Margined tortoise, *Testudo marginata*.

Margined Tortoise
Testudo marginata
SIZE: To 35 cm (14 in).
CHARACTERISTICS: Back edge of carapace strongly flared or rimmed and serrated.
DISTRIBUTION: Southern Greece; very warm, brushy slopes.
TEMPERATURE RANGE: 68–86°F (20–30°C).
WINTER HIBERNATION: Yes.
DIET: Primarily herbivorous (plant material); meat taken only occasionally.

Afghan Tortoise
Testudo horsfieldii
SIZE: To 20 cm (8 in).
CHARACTERISTICS: Carapace almost round; only four toes on each foot.

DISTRIBUTION: Iran, Afghanistan, Pakistan; dry steppe with low plant growth.
TEMPERATURE RANGE: 65–86°F (18–30°C).
WINTER HIBERNATION: Yes.
DIET: Primarily herbivorous (plant material).

Chaco Tortoise
Geochelone chilensis
SIZE: 20 cm (8 in) to 30 cm (12 in).
CHARACTERISTICS: "Parrot beak"—must NOT be trimmed; uniformly brownish.
DISTRIBUTION: Argentina, Paraguay; prairie, brush land, not quite as dry as in Mediterranean countries.
TEMPERATURE RANGE: 68–82°F (20–28°C).
WINTER HIBERNATION: No.
DIET: Primarily herbivorous (plant material).

Chaco tortoise, *Geochelone chilensis.*

Pancake tortoise, *Malacochersus tornieri*.

Pancake Tortoise
Malacochersus tornieri
SIZE: To 15 cm (6 in).
CHARACTERISTICS: The relatively soft and flexible carapace is normal; very flattened shape.
DISTRIBUTION: East Africa; dry, rocky regions with thorn bushes.
TEMPERATURE RANGE: 72–82°F (22–28°C).
WINTER HIBERNATION: No.
DIET: Herbivorous, but difficult to feed since the natural diet consists mainly of cacti.

Eastern Box Turtle
Terrapene carolina
SIZE: To 20 cm (8 in).
CHARACTERISTICS: Two hinges on plastron used for closing the shell tightly; legs and feet not as elephant-like as true tortoises.
DISTRIBUTION: Eastern United States; fields and forest margins, often close to water.
TEMPERATURE RANGE: 65–82°F (18–28°C).
WINTER HIBERNATION: Possible but not required (depends upon subspecies and origin of specimen).
DIET: Primarily herbivorous (plant material), but may take a bit of meaty foods.

Western box turtle, *Terrapene ornata.*

Western Box Turtle
Terrapene ornata
SIZE: To 15 cm (6 in).
CHARACTERISTICS: Like *Terrapene carolina*, but plastron with radiating yellow lines.
DISTRIBUTION: Great Plains and southwestern United States; drier habitats.
TEMPERATURE RANGE: 72–82°F (22–28°C).
WINTER HIBERNATION: May not be required.
DIET: Primarily herbivorous (plant material), but often takes much meaty foods.

BOX TURTLES are easy to recognize and often collectable in the United States. Their common name was derived from the presence of two hinges on the plastron (bottom shell) that are used to fold the anterior and posterior sections of the plastron upward, thus effectively closing the carapace like a box.
Unlike tortoises, box turtles need:
  —a waterproof terrarium (glass or plastic), as large as possible;
  —a heated bathing pool with easy access and egress;
  —opportunities to burrow into damp, warm soil or moss;
  —a dry sunning site;

—lots of live animal food, including earthworms, crickets, mealworms, and snails, as well as plant foods;

—as much fruit as possible, favorites determined by trial and error (my animals prefer kiwi fruit);

—lots of peace and quiet—the more the animals retreat into their shell the harder it is for them to adapt to captivity.

When the box turtle has settled down and adapted to captivity, we can simplify and to some degree even extend the care and maintenance program. For instance, in time many box turtles will learn to accept dog or cat food straight from the can, and they may even eat surprising amounts of this sort of food. It is easy to mix vitamin preparations and calcium powder into

Hatchling of a western box turtle.

such a mixture. Vitamin A is especially important because only this substance will inhibit eye infections.

In the middle of the summer box turtles can also be kept outdoors. For that purpose we must construct an outdoor enclosure much as for tortoises. However, this must always include a little pool (not merely a large water dish). These turtles usually behave quite differently outdoors than do tortoises. Most notably, they like to walk about in the rain! In fact, this is when they often go hunting for their favorite foods: earthworms and snails.

Admittedly, these brief hints on the care and maintenance of box turtles can not address all questions. Instead, they are meant to start you thinking and to stimulate your imagination. The fastest way for us to see whether we are doing the right things is to closely observe the reactions of our animals.

No matter where WE want to house tortoises, we must always take the silent wishes of our animals into close consideration. The question as to whether a particular type of housing is cheap or beautiful is of little relevance: first and foremost it must be appropriate for the species concerned! This involves ten specific prerequisites:

Housing

Heat

Tortoises are strongly dependent upon air and ground temperatures. Without adequate warmth there are no activities—no food intake, no digestion, no defecation. The optimum temperature range for the species mentioned in this book is about 65–86°F (18–30°C).

Shade

Too much heat is unhealthy even for tortoises. Their body must not be exposed to excessive heat over prolonged periods of time. Consequently, tortoises must be afforded shade or be given an opportunity to burrow.

Light

The tortoises discussed here will feed only during the hours of daylight. The minimum daily light requirement is 8 hours, preferably up to 12 hours.

Ultra-violet radiation

This must be provided at least intermittently so that the shell and bones become and remain firm. If the animals are kept outdoors the natural sunlight is sufficient. However, if the animals are being kept permanently indoors there must be supplementary UV radiation from a suitable fluorescent light.

FACING PAGE: A pile of straw can serve as bedding for a tortoise. Be sure the straw is dry, not wet or damp. Moldy straw is unhealthy, certain molds are harmful and attack the scales and soft parts of the body.

Dryness

Tortoises are sensitive to wetness. The substrate (ground) and sleeping site are only permitted to be slightly damp if they are also warm at the same time.

Space

Tortoises like to walk around for long periods of time. In cages that are too small they either become apathetic or they try to escape. The minimum space requirement for a small (baby) tortoise with a carapace length of up to 6 cm (2½ in) is 0.25 sq. meter (0.3 sq. yd.). An adult tortoise with a carapace length of 20 to 25 cm (8–10 in) should be given at least 2 sq. meters (2.4 sq. yd.). If several animals are kept, they need in excess of 10 sq. meters (12 sq. yd.). The animals will be even more comfortable if they are given two to five times as much space.

Sleeping site

Tortoises do not like to sleep in open, unprotected places. Darkness means protection to them, and protected areas must be provided even in captivity. They prefer a site where they can easily burrow, as into a pile of hay or straw. This site must be dry, warm, not be drafty.

Correct substrate

In the wild, tortoises walk over all sorts of terrain and burrow even into firm substrates. This does not injure them in any way. Quite to the contrary, the claws remain properly trimmed, the muscles are strengthened, and the animals are never bored. In captivity, however, unnatural or uniform substrates can easily lead to problems for tortoises. They tend to catch a cold on tiles or cold concrete. Rough and hard substrates tend to grind down the scutes and bones of the plastron and/or the claws wear down to the flesh of the feet. Smooth plastic, linoleum, and similar materials will cause their legs to slide to one side, leading to a deformed leg position; moreover, if the tortoise is turned over on its back it is no longer able to right itself.

Peat moss, sawdust, and sand are dangerous since the

Sheets of artificial turf make good substrates for tortoises. Such sheets come in a variety of sizes to fit a variety of enclosures and can be used over and over. Photo courtesy of Four Paws.

fine dust associated with these materials tends to get into the eyes and nose of tortoises and the food is also often contaminated by this dust. Ideal substrates are: grassy areas; medium size, round washed gravel; unfinished wood; natural sand stone tiles; and cork.

Involvement

Each animal must be able to use its intelligence. Apart from eating and sleeping, tortoises also like to keep busy. They explore new terrain, climb up to vantage points, and hunt for their own food. Climbing can be facilitated by putting two wooden boards end-to-end and placing a grass mat over this structure. Caution: This "lookout tower" must not be placed so it becomes an escape opportunity! To give the animals an opportunity to look for their own food one can cut out a few small sections of lawn with a spade and then place this into the tortoise enclosure. The animals will soon start grazing.

Protection against dangers

Nobody can expect tortoises to "know" what dangers lurk in strange new surroundings. Therefore, it is our responsibility to set up preventive measures. Some of the more common dangers include:

—A fall from a balcony is usually fatal because the carapace bursts open.

—Escaping from human care and attention is generally not rewarded with freedom; either the animal gets run over or it freezes to death during the next severe winter.

—Tying the animal up in a garden with a rope pulled through

Wild herons will not hesitate catching a pet tortoise that is left unattended in the backyard. Other larger predatory bird species can also eat tortoises and turtles.

Poinsettia is commonly found in many homes, not only during the holidays but all-year-round. Be sure this poisonous ornamental plant is not within reach of your tortoise.

a hole in the carapace is cruel. Tortoises never learn to accept such restraints. Moreover, in such a situation they are helplessly exposed to predatory birds.

—Large birds in general, such as ravens, crows, and some herons, are a real danger to tortoises. These are particularly aggressive during the nesting season when they have young and so require a lot of food. Consequently, tortoise meat is highly desirable to them at that time. Small tortoise are then carried away whole; larger ones are tossed on their back and the flesh is picked out of the carapace.

—Tortoises can suffer heat stroke far more readily than you may imagine on a very hot, exposed balcony, in a car parked in the sun, or in a pen without a shelter for shade.

—Environmental poisons, either natural ones or those spread by man, are very dangerous to tortoises; consequently, do not use snail bait, mouse poison, or insecticides around your house or garden. Make sure your animals do not have access to poisonous plants or their fruit, such as ivy, laurel, parson's hat, spurge, horse chestnut, yew tree, snow berry, fox glove, privet, lillies of the valley, laburnum, and many more. Among the indoor plants especially dangerous are oleander, wax flowers, stephanotis, and poinsettia.

With a few exceptions, there is really no reason tortoises may not be kept in a garden during appropriate weather. Below are two possible ways of housing tortoises in a garden.

Simple garden enclosure

Select a sunny section of lawn that is as large as possible. Its shape does not have to be square—quite to the contrary, broad angles are even better, because then courting males will not be able to jam weaker females into corners. Wooden posts are put into the ground every 2 m (6 feet) and at the corners. They should protrude about 25 cm (10 inches) above the ground. Then a shallow ditch is dug along the perimeter of the enclosure where the fence is going to be. The bottom piece of fencing timber is then laid into the ditch and nailed to the corner posts. The next piece of timber is nailed above the first one and so on until the corner post has been reached. Finally, a horizontal piece of timber protruding into the enclosure is nailed across the top of each side of the enclosure.

The cheapest material for such a fence is unfinished boards planed on one side only. These are usually the outer (half-round) section of logs. If the timber is to be coated against decay it must be done with a non-poisonous substance; most wood preservatives still give off poisonous substances after the smell is gone.

Other construction materials that can be used are concrete slabs and tiles, wire-reinforced glass, bricks or natural rock, old railway ties, and chicken wire. Whatever you use, never forget to install the horizontal retaining board at the top. This is the only reliable way of keeping tortoises from climbing out of a pen. In most cases the animals no longer want to escape because they cannot see the world beyond the fence so they have little desire to venture there.

Such a pen also needs a small protective shelter with an entrance hole. This can be of simple construction, but weather-proof materials must be used. The sloping roof should be covered with plastic sheeting or tar paper. It is of considerable advantage if one side of the roof is hinged and can be opened for cleaning and to check on the animals. An ample amount of dried leaves, hay, and straw for bedding is put into the shelter but must then be changed regularly. Finally, a shallow water dish (such as a bird bath) is set into the ground. A stone slab or tile or some small wooden boards nailed together

Housing

It is sensible to use a screen cover on your tank when housing your tortoise, not only to keep the tortoise from getting out but also to keep the insects used for feeding in. Photo courtesy of Four Paws.

serves a feeding station . . . and that's all there is to it! In order to provide protection against large birds (ravens, crows) the entire enclosure should be covered with a bird net (available from garden stores), especially if the tortoise is left unattended for some time.

Adult tortoise can stay in such an enclosure for most of the summer (depending upon your geographic location). It is, however, unsuitable for smaller tortoises, sick tortoises, and for all tortoises during wet and cold periods. Moreover, one has to expect that some specimens will try to burrow underneath the fence and escape. These problems can be avoided by making the following more complicated pen.

Enclosure with heating

You start out the same way you did before, but before the wooden fence is nailed down, a pit 50 cm (20 inches) wide, 1 to 2 meters (3–6 feet) long and about 15 cm (6 inches) deep is dug along the southern perimeter wall of the enclosure. Then the entire enclosed area is covered with plastic-coated mesh wire and the individual strips are tied together with wire. The wire mesh should go sufficiently beyond the perimeter lines so that it can be nailed from the outside against the lowest fence board. Finally the pit is filled in with a mixture of peat moss and sand. This is to stimulate the tortoises to deposit their eggs here and to serve as a burrowing area for the tortoises, since all other areas of the enclosure have no protective wire bottom.

After a short period of time grass will have grown through the wire mesh and render it essentially invisible. It is now easy for the animals to graze, but burrowing is restricted to one particular area. A simple protective shelter can be quickly converted into one that can be heated. An infra-red lamp is suspended from the gable of the shelter and connected through an underground cable to the nearest electricity supply. *CAUTION:* The cable must be encased in rubber; in order to protect it against mice and shovels, it is inserted inside an old garden hose. The disadvantage of the infra-red lamp is that only part of the floor area is heated. That spot will be occupied by the larger, more powerful animals, while the weaker ones are displaced to cold outer areas. It thus is better to have a shelter with floor heating, although this may be somewhat more expensive.

The basic shape of the shelter is box-like, with the sides sloped in such a way that a flat roof can be installed and then covered with plastic or tar paper. The entrance can be either in the front or at any of the sides, as required. A thick piece of styrofoam is placed on the bottom of the box and covered with three layers of extra-strength aluminum foil. Upon this we place thin wire mesh such as chicken wire. A heating cable such as is used for starting plants is then attached to this mesh by means of wire and string. This must be done in such a way that none of the heating coil loops come into contact

These hatchlings of the Greek tortoise required some heat in their holding cage or enclosure because they were hatched in very cold weather.

with each other (otherwise they will burn through). The heating coil is then covered by a strong, scratch-proof plate that must be a good heat conductor. The best (as well as the most expensive) is a thick sheet of aluminum. Thin concrete slabs, asbesto cement tiles, and special plastic sheets are also suitable.

All electric parts must be well covered and there must be no opportunity for the tortoises to come into contact with them. The danger of damaging the cable and giving both humans and tortoises a severe electrical shock is simply too great to be careless. There still remains the question when and how

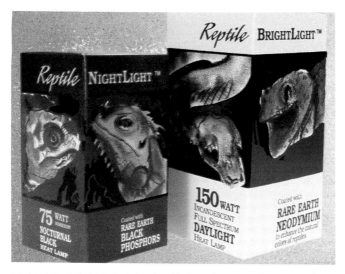

It is important that any tortoises kept indoors be exposed to proper photo-periods (day/light cycling) and adequate heat. With the correct types of bulbs, you can accomplish both. Check with your local pet shop for the types of bulbs required. Photo courtesy of Energy Savers.

the heat is turned on and off. This can, of course, be done man-ually (by hand), but this method is somewhat unreliable: if there is not enough heat the animals will suffer, if there is too much the electricity bill will sky-rocket. Therefore, I have sim-plified matters by installing a thermostat, but it is important to remember that the thermostat measures the air temperature *above* the tortoise and *not along the bottom.*This setup has worked very well for the animals as well as for their keeper. Nevertheless, for the dedicated tortoise fancier who is a "do-it-yourselfer" I would like to describe additional possibilities of how to technically perfect the tortoise enclosure.

Extras

In order to set up a BATHING POOL, a fairly deep hole has to be dug inside the enclosure (do not forget to cut the wire mesh first if it is on the ground). About two-thirds of the way up from the bottom place a few pieces of timber or iron rods across the pit. On top of this secure several layers of plastic sheeting and two or three layers of wire mesh. Then push a drain pipe through the middle of the plastic foil and wire mesh layers. With that in place, smear a thick layer of ready-mix concrete over the wire layer and around the drain pipe. Before the concrete has a chance to set, press some coarse gravel into it. This later will help the tortoises get out of the pool without difficulty. *IMPORTANT:* Make sure that the drain actually is located at the lowest point of the pool! Do not use an ordinary plug to close off the drain, because the tortoises will pull it out. Instead, an overflow pipe has proven to be very effective. Before the tortoises get access to their new pool, it should be left standing full of water for about a week. Then the pool is drained into the drainage pit every day for two or three days and refilled with fresh water via a garden hose. This should cleanse it of any chemicals in the concrete.

Shown is plastic sheeting utilized in the construction of a garden pool. Such a sheet can also be used in the building of a small bathing pool for tortoises.

A pool of water that is deep and has steep vertical sides can be dangerous to a tortoise. If unable to crawl out of the water, a tortoise will certainly drown.

The next luxury we may wish to provide for our tortoises could be a SUNBATHING SITE. Ideally suited for this is a narrow strip usually along the southern side of the enclosure. Several pieces of unfinished timber are nailed slightly obliquely across a couple of 2 × 4's. Each corner gets a post about 50 to 60 cm (20–24 inches) high supporting a frame made of 2 × 2's covered with louvered plastic panels like those used in greenhouses. A loose "curtain" made of greenhouse plastic that can be rolled down in front of the sunbathing site during periods of inclement weather completes the structure. This "solarium" now collects and retains every bit of sun and warmth. In essence this means that the animals can experience more "good weather" than is usual for northern latitudes.

Housing

A third luxury is the GRAZING PEN. It consists of a section of lawn such as is usually found in any garden. However, it must be made "escape-proof." In order to stop my tortoises from running away I have placed a series of short, round poles about 20 cm (8 inches) high spaced so that even the smallest tortoises would not fit through two adjacent poles even in an upright position. At the junction with the footpath I have placed a double set of poles into which a wide, thin piece of timber is inserted. A similar gate is installed at the regular enclosure and can be opened and closed as required. The animals

The red-footed tortoise, *Geochelone carbonaria*, is a species that can be purchased in the United States. The species is originally from northern South America.

are locked up in the enclosure every evening. They quickly adapt to this routine, and after a week they usually return to their shelter on their own to spend the night and sleep. The tremendous advantage of such grazing pens is that the animals always get enough fresh greens, which they clearly prefer over the cut, already wilted grass that they normally get. In addition, the tortoises can satisfy their wandering instinct. This is particularly important when "aggressive" males continually harass the females.

Keeping tortoises indoors

With a few exceptions, there is really no reason for keeping tortoises indoors during the summer. But during spring and fall it is necessary for climatic reasons to keep the animals inside. Moreover, sick, weak, and very young tortoises are often better housed inside than outdoors.

Tortoises should not be permitted to run freely inside an apartment. The floor is always too cold and is usually drafty. Instead, far more suitable are large aquaria, plastic tubs, wooden crates, and commercially available multipurpose cages. The ideal bottom substrate for these containers is rice straw mats. They retain the dirt without soiling the food and they can readily be thrown out and replaced with new ones. A cardboard box of appropriate size with a cut out as an entrance and with hay, straw, dried leaves, and moss as bedding is quite suitable for sleeping quarters. Food and water dishes must be made of earthenware or ceramics because these materials are more resistant than plastics.

Finally, we will need a piece of tree bark, a heavy branch, or something similar so the animals can climb. Actual size and installation depend on the size and strength of particular "climbers." (Yes, some tortoises do like to climb.) Weak and sick animals do not need a climbing facility.

Light and warmth can be provided by a desk or office lamp suspended above the floor in such a way that the largest animal can not reach it with its neck extended. The maximum temperature below the lamp should be about 95°F (35°C). A 60-watt bulb is usually already sufficient. Large cages will require two lamps, otherwise a large area of the cage will be too cold

A large aquarium will be adequate for housing a single tortoise or a box turtle as shown here. In addition to receptacles for food and water and the proper substrate, include a piece of wood on which a tortoise or turtle can climb.

and dark. If fluorescent lighting is used, an additional heat source still will have to be installed because fluorescent lights are so cool.

Flexible heating cables like those used for starting plants are adequate for heating indoor cages. The cable is placed in loops below the substrate or below the straw mat. It is important that individual loops do not come into contact with each other or with plastic or other inflammable materials! Cable

This red-footed tortoise, *Geochelone carbonaria*, while in captivity developed humps on the carapace. Specimens from the wild have smoother carapaces, without such strong humps. The cause is not known.

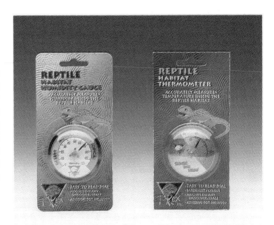

It is important to monitor the temperature of your tortoises home. Gauges and thermometers are available at your local pet shop. Photo courtesy of Ocean Nutrition.

wattage depends on the size of the area to be heated; an area of 60 cm × 60 cm (2 feet × 2 feet) needs about 40 watts. This type of heating is particularly suited for sick tortoises because it distributes heat into all corners of the cage. With this the animals can not crawl into a dark corner and cool down. If the tortoise requires heating in only part of the cage (if it is small but otherwise healthy, for instance) it is easier to use a heating pad sealed inside heavy non-flammable plastic. The lowest thermostat setting available usually provides just the right amount of heat.

Another type of heating involves the use of the so-called dark radiators. These are either porcelain bulbs or carbon arc lamps that give off little if any light. They fit into any standard light socket. They are not easy to find but may be available at pet shops that deal in reptiles and reptile accessories. They are screwed into any lamp socket like regular light bulbs and warm the cage from above.

With normal room temperatures of 68–72°F (20–22°C) all heaters should be turned off at night. Tortoises need a day/-night rhythm, and only sick ones must be given constant 24-hour heat until they are fully recovered.

Diet

Tortoises are almost always omnivorous, so it is no problem at all to feed them a highly varied diet. It is, however, imperative that you discard the old notion that one lettuce leaf per day per animal is sufficient! Although lettuce is very popular with tortoises and it does contain many vitamins, it does not contain them all and has barely any minerals and no protein. The most significant component of a tortoise is its carapace, which consists primarily of minerals and proteins. Consequently, these animals require not only plant material as food, but also eggs, meat, cottage cheese, or—better yet—earthworms, snails, and other small animals.

Fortunately, active tortoises are extremely curious about anything edible. They smell it and, if it is suitable, taste it. What then follows is decisive as to whether a particular type of food has a "future" or not:

—spitting out the food: food rejected;
—walking away from it after a couple of bites: not entirely to its liking;
—actively feeding on it.

You can and should experiment with the diet's composition, especially since each animal has its preferences and dislikes, and even this pattern can change from one month to the next.

It is virtually impossible to force a tortoise to eat a particular type of food that it dislikes. Stubbornness is one of the most obvious traits of a tortoise! Animals that have been kept alone often stubbornly insist on certain foods—and don't care how nutritionally inadequate these may be. In this case, of course, food envy, the natural teacher, does not come into play. Yet tortoises—even solitary specimens—can be fooled into taking a mash mixture. The recipe is as follows: Take the known favor-

FACING PAGE: A completely soft diet for tortoises is not healthy. In order to keep the beaks in good condition, a tortoise must tear rough and tough food apart.

ite food item and macerate it into a mash. Add to this increasing amounts of supplements, such as vitamin drops, calcium powder, cottage cheese, and meat. This little trick tends to work rather well as long as the "favorite" can still be tasted.

Some tortoises seem to know when they are lacking something nutritionally and also know exactly what is missing. They tend to chew on entire cuttlefish bones for budgies and parrots, hunt for earthworm and snails that happen to appear quite by chance, and make monumental efforts to reach certain plants that have grown over the fence from next door. The behavior of tortoises in fields and pens with a rich herbal fauna is very conspicuous. Quite obviously the animals are looking for only certain leaves, those that they like and are good for them.

On the other hand, some tortoises seem to prefer to lose weight rather than taking any natural or artificial remedies against their deficiency problems. These are the animals that benefit most from the "mash" of their favorite food and supplements. This way many tortoises have been made to eat something that they would have normally refused.

When in season, snails can be collected in numbers and given to a tortoise. The shell is also a source of useful minerals and salts.

Specialty tortoise foods have been made available to the hobbyist. You can find these foods at your local pet shop. Photo courtesy of Ocean Nutrition.

Mashes

Mash mixtures are not only for "tricking" tortoises into eating what's good for them, but they are also very popular. The basis for these mixtures can be rice mash, semolina, water-soaked dry bread, oatmeal, kibble for dogs, whole-grain pastas, or ground barley. The additives include cooked fruits and vegetables including the broth (in an emergency use canned products), freshly mashed fruit, tomatoes, cottage cheese, eggs, minced meat, chopped up nettles, and—as a vitamin-rich "spice"—parsley. There are virtually no limits on our imagination. Only real spices are not allowed for tortoises! Salt should be used very sparingly. As long as the mash mixture is not covered with fungus or has started to rot, it is edible. Many combinations are possible, even cherries with parsley and minced meat with bananas.

Even the most delicious mash mixture is not suitable as the main or sole diet. It is soft and uniform, so it does not offer an opportunity for the animals to wear down their horny jaw sheaths. The consequence of this is that often a "parrot beak" condition begins to develop and the jaws must be trimmed—and who can open the tightly closed mouth of a strong, healthy tortoise without injuring the animal? Therefore, prevention is better than cure. The mash mixture should be fed only about twice a week. The rest of the time the tortoises must get things they can chew and pull on.

Green Foods

A list of herbs, fruits, and vegetables suitable for tortoises is long. Also long would be the list of all those poisons commonly found on these food items. I can no longer in good conscience recommend to anybody that they collect dandelions from a field or lawn. After all, this could be adjacent to a field where highly potent poisonous substances have been sprayed. Even the outer leaves of lettuce and cabbage from our kitchen should not be used as animal food if these items have been grown under normal agricultural routines. The outer leaves are the site where most residual herbicides are retained.

You can really be safe only with green food that is home-grown. The ideal situation is a clean garden that is set up as a pen, with some beet and lettuce plants and a few other vegetables and fruit bushes and trees. Surrender in your fight against daisies, dandelions, clover, crowfoot, speedwell, and plantain. Save on fertilizer, weed killer, and weekly lawn mowing. Simply build a fence around this new pen (a part of your lawn or garden) and let your tortoises "graze." The tortoises really will not be able to keep the herbs and grass down (they are not too fond of them anyway), but at least we will not have to worry about green food all summer long. Select the best fruits and vegetables (i.e., those without aphids) for yourself and let the rest, including the weeds, go to the tortoises! You will find that there are no tortoises in better condition than those that have been grazing in a poison-free garden for most of the gardening season. Under these circumstances the only supplemental food required is some minced meat with calcium powder given once a week—and all the work is done!

Anyone who does not have a garden will have to make-do with store-bought green feed. Thoroughly washed lettuce, different types of cabbage, peeled tomatoes, and peeled fruit (the skin contains the highest concentration of poisonous substances sprayed!) will do. However, I purchase carrots (which are excellent food either raw and grated or cooked whole) only when they are organically grown because carrots remove a lot of poisonous substances from the soil that neither can be washed off nor peeled away. Some types of vegetables, such as beans or cauliflower, usually are eaten by tortoises only

Diet

when cooked (the water from this is very useful for making a mash). All fruit must be ripe or even over-ripe but must not carry fungus or have started to decay. Fruits with firm flesh—such as apples and pears—should be grated or finely chopped. Melons are cut into large pieces but NOT peeled (the only exception!). The animals like to chew the melon pieces all the way down to the tough skin, which is good for their horny-rimmed jaws.

Most authorities on animal feeding recommend the boiling of slugs before feeding to a tortoise or turtle.

Feeding Times

If your tortoises are not permitted to gather most of their own food, you should get them used to fixed feeding times. Feeding must be at least once a day, either late morning or the afternoon. You will quickly notice that these are periods when the animals are particularly active. The feeding site should be protected against rain. Food dishes are not particularly useful; by and large, tortoises tend to take food away from each other (food envy).

I can not give a rule for the amounts of food that have to be given, such as one animal of a certain weight must be given so much food. However, in a general way it can be said:
— fat tortoises get green food once daily and lots of hard food so that they have to "work";
— thin tortoises get high-calorie vitamin-rich mash mixtures given alternately with fruit. They should be given food as often as they want, but at least twice a day!

A part from minor ailments, the health status of tortoises in captivity is generally rather stable, provided *excellent* care and maintenance are given. The word "excellent" should be emphasized! In any event, this is invariably easier and more desirable than even the most perfect disease treatment. Apart from proper care, the close and continuous observation of the animals is also an essential ingredient in disease prevention. Diseases detected early are only half as difficult to cure as chronic cases. Once a general weakness and circulatory problems have joined the actual disease symptoms of a simple cold or diarrhea, then the prospects of a cure become increasingly remote. Eventually then the animal reaches the dreaded stage where it is no longer capable of absorbing and storing warmth.

Diseases

The following basic rules must be applied as quickly as possible:

RULE I: Diseased and/or weakened tortoises require continuous exposure to about 86°F (30°C) heat for a complete cure. Therefore, they should be kept in an enclosure with floor heat and an illumination of at least eight hours per day.

RULE II: Never apply the "do-or-die" method. Prolonged periods of starvation weaken the animal and damage its gastro-intestinal system.

For a non-feeding tortoise I usually resort very early on to force-feeding. For that I use a one-way syringe (without needle) available from your veterinarian or reptile specialty suppliers. The syringe is filled with a highly nutritious mash mixture of baby food and various protein extracts (available from drug stores or health food shops). Depending upon the suspected cause of the disease, I then add:

—10 drops of a vitamin supplement;

—10 drops broad-spectrum antibiotic;

—an appropriate amount of laxative or antidiarrhetic;

—and/or 10 drops of a circulatory support medication (see your veterinarian).

The general health of a tortoise can be judged by the condition of its beaks, mouth, tongue, and above all by its appetite.

This mixture is then force-fed to the animal. The weaker the animal the smaller the amount given per feeding, yet the more frequent the feedings must be.

The forcible opening of a tortoise's mouth requires a bit of practice because the animal will resist this procedure violently as long as it has any strength left at all. First and foremost, it is important to secure the head. If the animal is suspicious it will retract its head and only a little trick will coax it out again. Hold the animal up side down for a short period of time; the animal will soon attempt to change this uncomfortable position and the head will reappear. We then reach from above with thumb and index finger laterally behind the animal's cheek bones and so prevent a renewed head retraction. Gently force the mouth open with a fingernail of the right hand (never use a metal instrument for that purpose!) and then quickly insert a free finger of the left hand between the jaws. Now we take the previously prepared food syringe and squirt the mixture into the mouth, but not too deeply. As soon as the mouth slams shut some of the mash will be forced out again, but this does not matter. However, it is important to check whether the remainder has indeed been swallowed. Some animals will simply wait until they are returned to their cage and spit it out again. Swallowing movements can be seen along the ventral side of the neck. Swallowing can be further aided by gentle massage (in the abdominal direction) along the underside of the neck.

As long as the animal can be force-fed it needs to be force-fed. When healthier, the patient will decide to eat on its own. Indeed, the animal should be tempted to do that as often and in as many ways as possible. This is far better than any force-feeding!

If a tortoise is already so weak that continuous heat and force-feeding do not bring the desired results, then the third basic rule is applied.

RULE III: Seek professional veterinary care. Only a veterinarian can administer many injections, and an injected medication always works faster than one that has been administered orally. Injections are given subcutaneously (under the thin skin) along a hind leg.

As long as you use the medications listed in this book, their usefulness outweighs any inherent dangers. You should, however, be very cautious with antibiotics, sulfonamides, and anesthetics that have not been sufficiently tested on tortoises! Many of them will not work and instead will induce an often fatal incompatibility shock.

When faced with difficult disease questions it is recommended that you seek expert veterinary advice, preferably from a veterinarian who has experience with tortoises. This can be a zoo veterinarian, the closest veterinary clinic, or a veterinarian associated with a university. When you get your tortoise you might want to call several of your local veterinarians to see which of them could deal with a sick tortoise.

Substrates can play an important role in helping to keep your terrarium free from disease. Certain types are specially processed to eliminate parasites. Photo courtesy of Four Paws.

COMMON AILMENTS

Eye infection

CAUSE: Mechanical damage; infection; vitamin deficiency.

TREATMENT: Bathe eye with camomile tea, followed by topical application of eye ointment (see your veterinarian). Supplement with high dosages of vitamin A daily.

CHANCES OF RECOVERY: Very high, provided the cornea (eyeball) has not been destroyed.

Intestinal prolapse

CAUSE: Unknown. Can not be cured.

TREATMENT: Apply antibiotic ointment to protruding intestinal tissue in order to firm up tissue. Must not be allowed to dry out. See your veterinarian.

Diarrhea

CAUSE: Incorrect diet, especially decaying or fermenting foods, or lettuce followed by lactose (milk-like) foods; worms.

Scenic sheeting placed on the back of a tortoise's tank will create the illusion of depth and add a nice visual touch. Such sheets come in a variety of tableaux and can be purchased at many pet shops.

TREATMENT: Let the animal fast for two days if it is not too weak. Then give mixture of baby food together with black tea, camomile tea, and some laxative powder. Later give some watery rice paste, grated carrots, bananas, and fresh willow tree leaves. Send out fresh feces samples for an examination for the presence of worms.

CHANCES OF RECOVERY: Very good if the cause has been determined early enough and treatment is initiated in time. If the intestinal tract has already sustained serious damage the animals can be kept alive only with difficulty and by means of a strict, life-long diet.

Iron deficiency

CAUSE: Unbalanced iron-deficient diet.

TREATMENT: In less serious cases give an iron preparation used for children mixed in with the food or given as drops administered directly into the mouth of the tortoise. Serious cases require two or three injections of an iron preparation administered by a veterinarian. This is followed by continuous administration of the children's iron preparation mixed in with the food. Give spinach.

Diseases

Colds and/or respiratory ailments
CAUSE: Cold; dampness; drafts; infection.

TREATMENT: Keep the animal in warm environment. Do not waste time with home treatment; seek immediate veterinary care for administration of antibiotic injections. Keep animal warm and dry and avoid any drafts.

CHANCES OF RECOVERY: Very good. Avoid relapses.

Paralysis
CAUSE: Unknown; possibly vitamin deficiency.

TREATMENT: Seek immediate veterinary attention. Keep the animal warm. Cut food into small pieces so that the animal does not have to exert itself feeding.

CHANCES OF RECOVERY: Reasonably good if caught during initial stages of the disease.

Carapace scaling
CAUSE: Possibly fungi.

TREATMENT: Remove loose flakes from the upper carapace layer and apply fungicide to the affected areas below. Do not overlook cracks, otherwise the disease will continue to spread.

CHANCES OF RECOVERY: Good, but damage to carapace remains permanently visible.

Any of the horny scales that fall off on account of fungal infection will not regenerate, thus exposing the bones of the carapace as illustrated here.

Carapace softening and deformities

CAUSE: Calcium and vitamin deficiency; incorrect diet; not enough UV radiation.

TREATMENT: Add calcium to the food in the form of ground-up egg shells, cuttlefish bone, or calcium tablets. In addition, give 1–4 drops calcium supplement in the food or directly into the mouth, at first every day, later once a week. As soon as the carapace has firmed up, UV radiation once a week is sufficient.

CHANCES OF RECOVERY: Good, but the rachitic deformities never disappear. In serious cases they may even inhibit any further growth of the animal.

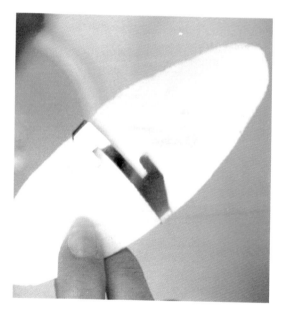

Cuttlefish bone for birds is sold in pet shops. It can be pulverized or ground-up and included with the mash mixture for tortoises. Some tortoises ignore cuttlefish bone that is intact.

Parrot beak

CAUSE: Not enough solid food.

TREATMENT: Careful trimming of horny cutting edges back into the natural form by using nail clippers or small wire cutters. Smooth the cuts by using a fine nail file. Be careful not to damage the tongue!

CHANCE OF RECOVERY: Not a permanent condition.

Diseases

Poisoning

CAUSE: Feeding on poisonous plants or snails that have ingested snail bait.

TREATMENT: If poisoning is suspected give crushed tablets of thistle (health food store) together with a little food or water. In addition, give heavy vitamin supplements. Not effective in very serious cases of poisoning.

Constipation

CAUSE: Incorrect diet; lack of exercise; damage to gastro-intestinal system through medication.

TREATMENT: Feed head lettuce. Possibly some laxative tea given directly into the mouth of the animal. Daily baths in lukewarm water, for up to 1½ hours. Induce exercising.

CHANCE OF RECOVERY: Very good.

Vitamin deficiency

CAUSE: Incorrect diet.

TREATMENT: For one week, daily multivitamin preparation given directly into the mouth or with food. IMPROVE THE DIET!

CHANCE OF RECOVERY: Good, as long as there has not been any permanent damage.

The following vitamins occur naturally in the substances listed below:

—Vitamin A: In parsley, spinach, fresh eggs, fresh fish liver, generally in green plant parts.
—Vitamin B: In fresh liver, peas, beans, yeast, vegetable oils, and generally in green plant parts.
—Vitamin C: In parsley, oranges, strawberries, red and black currants, kiwi fruit, cabbage.
—Vitamin D: Can be formed in the digestive tract by intestinal flora. Also found in cabbage, liver, spinach, parsley, tomatoes, strawberries, and green lettuce.

Worms

CAUSE: Infection (fecal contamination) with worm eggs from infected tortoises, contaminated food and from soil of the enclosure. Have fresh feces checked for the presence of worms and/or eggs.

The soft tissue of the plastron, like the hinge of this box turtle, is quite delicate and is subject to abrasions, punctures, and lacerations.

TREATMENT: See your veterinarian for a safe and effective wormer after a stool examination has shown what type of worm is present. Follow manufacturer's instructions exactly.

CHANCE OF RECOVERY: Good. Reinfection must be prevented. This means that cages, food dishes, and water bowls must be washed with a disinfectant. A garden enclosure must be dug up or covered with worm-free top soil.

Injuries to carapace

CAUSE: Usually through lawn mower or shovel damage to partially or completely buried or hidden animals.

TREATMENT: Injuries affecting only the horny and bony layers of the carapace should be covered with antibiotic ointment. Injuries to the plastron must also be protected with a gauze or plaster dressing. Wounds extending into the flesh must be treated by a veterinarian. The affected animals should be kept indoors to prevent maggot infestation.

CHANCE OF RECOVERY: Very good with proper care if injuries are not severe.

Diseases

Wounds

CAUSE: Mechanical damage from nails, screws, metal parts, wire, or splinters; wedged or torn off claws; repeated rough copulation attempts by males; development of intestinal fistulas in older females when intestine is damaged through laying eggs.

TREATMENT: Apply antibiotic ointment to simple wounds. Pus-filled wounds must be cleaned with sterile instruments. Use gauze, not cotton wool, for cleaning wounds, then apply antibiotic ointment and cover (if possible) with gauze and plaster dressing.

CHANCE OF RECOVERY: Very good, if treatment is repeated and is kept up sufficiently long.

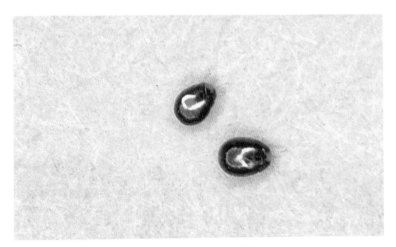

Ticks when engorged with blood become very visible.

Ticks

The tissue damage caused by ticks can be subject to secondary bacterial infections. Ticks must never be simply ripped off the host. Instead, an application of salad oil or a drop of nail polish will cause the tick to suffocate and it then lets go of the host on its own, at least in theory. Actually, many ticks hold on regardless of any oils put on them and must eventually be pulled off. Antibiotic ointment can be applied to the wound.

In their native countries tortoises "go to sleep" when the environmental conditions become unfavorable for a length of time. This does not have to be in the winter. For instance, during the summer it can get so hot and dry that tortoises bury themselves in damp, cool soil. Such extreme warmth and dryness usually do not occur in northern latitudes, and we do not have to simulate these hot conditions since any hibernation (called estivation in summer) during the summer is not necessary for the well-being of the animals.

Over-Wintering

Normal winter hibernation (or over-wintering) is a vastly different story. It is triggered by ambient temperatures that are so low that the tortoises are no longer able to move or feed. At that point the tortoises will bury themselves in the ground, using their last remaining strength. Then their bodies become rigid and all vital functions, such as heartbeat and respiration, work only in slow-motion; the utilization of nutrients is correspondingly small.

Tortoises that are able to over-winter correctly rarely lose any weight. They are then well-rested next spring. Susceptibility to diseases is reduced, and the desire to reproduce is greater. The mortality among tortoises that have been properly over-wintered is in the long term lower than among tortoises that remain "awake" throughout the year.

Keeping tortoises awake should be an exceptional situation. Sick and weak animals must not be permitted to hibernate; instead, they must be nursed in an indoor cage with lots of light and heat. It is, however, important to remember that tortoises during the winter always eat less than during the summer. Then there are those tortoises that simply do not seem to be able to hibernate. The cause for this is quite often prolonged warm weather periods or the animals have been kept too warm indoors. Apart from that there may also be other factors that are either unknown or uncontrollable. There is no alternative

In northern latitudes a Greek tortoise will have no desire to sleep in the summer months because the ambient temperature is not as warm as that prevailing in its area of distribution, Greece and adjacent territories.

but to keep such "restless wanderers" warm through the winter, with lots of light and good food. After all, the only possibilities that exist are hibernating, with little nutrient utilization, and not hibernating, with a normal food supply.

Large tortoises can be permitted to hibernate for five months, from the beginning of November until the end of March, but not longer. This is a good period since there is hardly any good food around for tortoises. Unfortunately, in northern climates tortoises can not remain outdoors until the end of October. From September onward they need a warm indoor facility where they can put on extra weight.

Individual tortoises can be accommodated in a large wooden crate with a lamp suspended above. If there are more animals they will require a larger facility. For that purpose I have equipped old tables in my basement with upright plank edges to restrain the animals. Each of these temporary enclosures has floor heat over more than one-third of its floor area. This third has been darkened and is filled with straw. The remainder of the area is covered with newspaper and/or rice mats and is illuminated and heated by two lamps. Here is where they feed and wander about a little.

It is imperative that cages that are kept in the basement should never be placed on the cold floor. It would be impossible to provide adequate heat under such conditions. Cleanliness is equally important. When the animals are forced to run constantly through a food-feces-urine mixture they get not only dirty but wet and cold also. Therefore, I do not give any water to my animals in the basement, but I do offer fresh green food instead.

Years ago I used to keep all tortoises in the same "temporary" cage. Not only was this too small, but with a normal diet and lots of heat the males would continue their noisy, amorous pursuits of the females until the temperature dropped. The females were helplessly exposed to courting males in these tight quarters, and they invariably preferred to retreat into the straw rather than being beaten up at the food dish. Now I keep males and females in separate cages and all animals go into hibernation much more calmly. The noise level in the basement has dropped considerably!

This is my step-by-step over-wintering procedure. At the end of October feeding ceases from one day to the next. The light and heat remain on for the time being. The tortoises

Ventral aspects of a male (left) and a female (right) Greek tortoise. The recognition of the sexes becomes important if the sexes have to be kept apart during over-wintering.

are now bathed in shallow, luke-warm water every other day until the greenish brown feces has cleared from the intestine. This can take up to an hour (white mucus originates from the bladder and does not count). After the bath the animal is carefully dried off and returned to the warm cage. This entire procedure must be repeated three or four times until the intestine is definitely empty! This is of great importance since it is the factor that determines whether an animal is going to survive the over-wintering process. Food remnants in the digestive tract would decay during the winter, causing death.

Once the "bathing week" has been completed, the heat is turned off. At that point I clean the temporary winter quarters and fill them up with straw. Alternatively, you can set up small sleeping boxes, using dry leaves and moss as bedding.

61

Peat moss and sawdust are unsuitable because the fine dust from these substances tends to settle in the eyes and lungs of the tortoises.

Tortoise fanciers sometimes slightly dampen the bedding inside the sleeping boxes from time to time. Many swear by this method. I do not! With a relative humidity of 65% in the basement the danger of desiccation is minor. With too much dampness there is a very real danger of the development of fungus. Just as important as the humidity is the temperature in the basement. During hibernation the temperature should be between 36°F and 50°F (2–10°C). Below 36°F (2°C) the danger of freezing becomes real; above 50°F (10°C) there is a slight "coming to" among the tortoises. A suspicious shuffling inside the straw bedding indicates that they are slowly moving. When there is movement there is an energy requirement, and this is one thing hibernating animals must use very sparingly.

I have observed in my animals that they tend to lose a lot of weight at temperatures close to 50°F (10°C); however, at average temperatures of 41–46°F (5–8°C) they still have almost the same weight in spring as they did in autumn.

In order to monitor temperature and humidity in the basement two instruments should be purchased: a hygrometer, which indicates humidity in %, and a maximum-minimum thermometer. The later not only shows the current temperature level, it also indicates what variations (up or down) took place. Without these instruments on hand you can use the following general rule: if potatoes can be stored in the basement without problems, it is also suitable for hibernating tortoises.

Once hibernation comes to an end, whether naturally or induced by the keeper, the animals initially are kept only under light and with adequate warmth. After one or two days the animals will come back to life. Then they have to be bathed again extensively. They will also drink copious amounts of water. This is very important: the water fills the gastro-intestinal system with liquid and stimulates the internal organ systems to renewed full activity so that (first and foremost) gastric juices and enzymes are produced again. Only AFTER this has taken place can we resume feeding.

The following books by T.F.H. Publications are available at pet shops everywhere.

TURTLES AND TERRAPINS:
A Complete Introduction By Jo Cobb
Hardcover **CO-026**
Softcover **CO-026S**

A Completely illustrated, completely practical guide to keeping shelled reptiles of all types successfully, from housing and feeding

SUGGESTED READING

to health care and breeding. Dozens of common species are discussed.

5½ x 8½; 128 pages.
Illustrated with 91 full-color photos and 14 full-color line drawings.

ENCYCLOPEDIA OF TURTLES
By Dr. Peter C. H. Pritchard (H-1011)
Contents: Turtle Identification. Turtle Structure and Function. Turtle Evolution and Fossil History. Emydid Turtles. Land Tortoises. Mud, Musk, and Snapping Turtles. Soft-Shelled Turtles, Monotypic Turtle Families. Sea Turtles. Side-Neck Turtles. Turtle Conservation and Exploitation. Turtles in Captivity. Two Appendices. Glossary.
Audience: This book is of value to pet keepers, scientific turtle experts, and everyone in between, being particularly mindful of the intelligent general naturalist and the academic zoologist who has use for an overview of the turtles within the covers of a single volume.
Illustrated with 358 color photos, 304 black and white photos, 70 line drawings; Hardcover; 5½ x 8½, 896 pages.

Index

Page numbers printed in **bold** face refer to photographs.